JOY OF BEING

VeerajaR

FIRST EDITION

2013

Cover Graphics and Book Design: VeeraMahal Consulting

Indie Publishing via Create Space

Printed in the United States of America

ISBN-10: 1484086260
ISBN-13: 978-1484086261

JOY OF BEING

JOY OF BEING

Poetry for the Heart, Mind and Spirit

VeerajaR

JOY OF BEING

"Life is joyful!
However, at times… life gets tough,
challenging and is often beyond our control.
Faith helps us endure—just as in the
metamorphosis of a butterfly—to emerge,
beautiful in spirit."

To emerge—

To love, to laugh

Oh, how joyful!

To be free—

To grow in faith

Oh, how blissful…

To morph in spirit

To emerge, anew!

—VeerajaR

DEDICATION

To Augustine…
My shining armor and husband!

FOREWORD

VeerajaR writes in awe of the beauty of the world and the joy of being. As a scientist, she understands the physical realities of our planet; as a poet, she composes with ardor about the gifts and love of God; and as an artist, she reveals the harmonies of color and place. Her poetry and images spring from both the Tennessee beauty around her and the rich culture of her youth in Ceylon. The lush world of the tropics and the inner feelings of the human heart infuse her work.

In one poem, she revels in the beauty of sunrise, wishing that the sense of joy and peace will permeate all, and the distant "deserts and war struck" places be touched by that same glow of peace in its passing. In others she embraces the beauty and yearnings of human spirit; challenges the worldly constraints that limit hope and faith. Through these poems, she lifts our hearts with hope and joy, often holds out the promise of a union with Divine Being, an ultimate resolution.

Her God is One, her sense of place is global, all are part of each; VeerajaR can render into poetry both the fragment and the whole.

Sally R. Lee, PhD.

JOY OF BEING

CONTENTS

*Refer to Author Notes (pg.102)

Poetry for the Heart, Mind and Spirit

VeerajaR

IN PRAYER...

GOOD MORNING
IN GOD

As sun gleams its rays and

Dawn reveals the new day

"Good Morning" I want to say

To all… have a good day —

In GOD, every day —

I meant to say!

(Foremost)

I submit to YOU… my day

Help me keep all evil at bay

GOD! Ground me in You, I pray.

Your PEACE in me You display

For YOUR will every day—

Use me — YOU may!

Good Morning! I want to say

To all come across my way

With smile radiating laser ray

Healing hurts and hatred nay

"Have a GOD's day"—

I yearn to say!

With every brush stroke, a

Rainbow I want displayed

Over the deserts and war struck

Removing all pain and dismay

GOD's Peace today — and

Always — I want to say!

Grace of GOD

From me

How these verses flow

Free as a river, I do not know

But,

I feel the joyous duty is mine

To share God's grace thus shine!

VeerajaR

IN AWE...

Promise

Brightest Sun to…

Light the days - why

Mighty dark of night

Moon rays?

Rhythms of night

Days to years - how

Rhythms of heart

Beat for years?

Timeless Dance

From the One

Who maketh thine

Atoms' core and danceth within

But,

Extends beyond the galactic spins

To timeless stillness that sustains

From Him

Created you and me, thus

Taketh form in visible space

But,

At heart ticking is His grace

To dance in joyful life with peace!

In Awe

Are

Cardinal red and cawing Blue Jay…

Golden Finch to green Parrot,

Brush strokes of Joy

from

Almighty's palette?

Are

Fluttering butterflies

Spotted and striped,

Flowing designs

from...

God's kaleidoscope?

Share One Earth

We are all the same

Deep down in the heart

We all seek happiness

But go different routes

We yearn for Peace

Wish for Heavenly bliss, yet

We fight each other… in

Endless—pointless—battles!

Green and blessed earth… one

Together that we share

Land that is divided, but

Joined by the oceans, one.

One moon for the night for all

One sun to share with all!

Help raise one another

All nations—not just us!

Echoes In The Heart

In our heart is where

In every corner… of

The chambers, echoes

The truth from where

In comes the spirit

Into living being!

In every beat of my heart

Innervated are my likings:

Scents of sea breeze and jasmine

Sweet red cherries and mangosteen

Love for reading and nature's beauty

Loyalty to God, my family and country!

In our heart's fibers

In ticking muscle and nerve

Purkinje's, moment zero to

Surge of every joy in essence

Finely embedded beyond

Fine science could ever unravel!

In my heart lies

Innocent dreams that

Brought me pieces of heaven,

Butterflies and wishes to fingertips.

Transplant my heart if in need

Transpire my joy to another and all!

Boundless

Barely heeding any worry

Growing aglow in tropical haven,

Nature abound with smiles - to

Nurture and rule young souls…

Bare little feet

Chasing waves and kites around

Ancient Ceylon's boundless beach

Was our heavenly playground!

Thousand Names

You are my brother, my sister

Yellow, brown, black or white…

We are all one.

When you succeed

We… too, are lifted. For

We are all children of God!

Though thousand names

We call him… Almighty is one!

Hallowed heaven will come down

Knocking at our doors

When we understand

GOD IS ONE and ONLY!

By thousand names

We may call Him. Know

He is one—the

Almighty… Creator of us all!

The Source

What makes you feel…

What comes out at the tip of my brush or

What pours out of the nib of my pen - is

What I have created?

What made me my mother's daughter...

What makes you see and hear

What awe I felt within my soul - for

What I am blessed to be?

What angel you'd be and

What that I am and would be,

What good we'd be... is all

What our God wishes to be!

For Reader Reflections "In Awe"

IN SEARCH...

The Quest

Aren't we mere travelers?

Just passing by?

Why? Oh, Why?

Then we carry

More… then worry

When surely,

We are not here

to stay?

Travel where and Why?

We search...

And we search

Find trust, friends

Family and life

But, Alas!

It's time again…

To travel!

The Rat Race

Where *to* we rush everyday

Care not even to pray

Soaring sales and money pays

Power or poverty leading the way

Hours squeezed out of the day

Poor souls we lost the ways!

Freedom

Oh! In shimmering self-made cage

Of steaming jealousy and scourging rage

Over-possessiveness and growing greed

Objects immaterial that steadily feed

Our ego, poor souls – thus, trapped!

Open the ugly cage, so... warped

Out let pure souls free to be

One with loving GOD, Almighty!

Oh, I AM

"I AM who I AM"

With Thee, all I am

Who I am!

From dust to dust, am I

Your song and dance… of

Joy, I AM?

"I AM who I AM"

Without Thee… Oh, I AM

Who I am?

VeerajaR

The Lost

What makes a heart so very lost?

That blinds wide-eyes so shut... of

What angelic little faces so pure

Might only levitate, but (shot) no more!

Humanity

Without fire

Shines no pure gold

Without pain

Beats no loving heart

Without faith

Rejoices no true soul

Without God

Spared no humanity!

Essence of Being

Would I have known…

Who I am – if You

My God hadn't whispered

My name to my very being!

Would I have felt…

What love is – if you

My mother hadn't held

Me, close to your heart!

Would I have known...

What I could be – if you

My love hadn't held

My arms at the altar!

Would I have known...

Who I am – if you

My babies hadn't blessed

Me, with your being!

For Reader Reflections "In Search"

VeerajaR

IN HOPE...

Old Couple

How old could you be…

Just so yonder

How many storms and cold winters

Thou two have weathered

I do wonder

Bowing not of old age, but of love still tender

Show of strength and endurance

I ponder

Now and forever

Bowing to God's plan, you do inspire!

Never Far Away

Your thoughts

Lost in the turmoil of

Worldly demands today

May be far away, from

The one gave birth to you

While lying alone

In the hospital bed…

Your thoughts, mother

While lying alone

In the hospital bed, today

Is far away with

Those you gave birth to, now

Lost in the turmoil of

The worldly demands…

Goodbyes can wait

Goodbyes can wait…

Take their time, lost

In the busy wide world

Buying time for breaking hearts or

Bringing hope for purposeful lives, but

All I want today is to hold your hands

Look you in the eye and tell you…

How much I love you!

Wings

The pain searing deep, wrench

Your body riddled with wretched wounds

Emptiness welling up in your heart

Echoing universal questions that surge

    Oh, God! Why? Why me?

    What have I done to deserve this?

Every deep tear that scarred your heart

Every writhing pain you overcame, burnt

Into misery wrinkles on your forehead. But,

I see compassion surge for others hurt

Impatience left space anew for wisdom

Imbibed in your heart lifted to my kingdom!

And beside you I Am, trust

All the way and every tough test

Every wound and scar—a beautiful spot

Every wise-wrinkle, a colorful stripe

To adorn your churning soul to glow

To emerge in heaven, your wings to grow!

The Loss: A Mother's Cry

The person you did not become

And the life taken away – for

you…

I cry, from the depths of my

soul

And will weep from within my

grave!

Bullets

Bullets filled with simply love

Could also pierce iron clad hearts

But would shed no precious life

Only, forever sustained hurt…

Bullets of love sheathed in hope

Could also to targets swoop

But would lift crushed-spirits so high

Only happiness limited to sky!

Bullets of love and hope in all

Could also heal wounds too old

But for rage and despair to deplete

Only required is a weapon of peace!

I Wish

I wish I can heal your pain

That I feel deep in my heart

Lost for words, I sob—for you

Lost have we a caring one!

I wish I can stop your tears

Make it all go away

And grant you a wish—for you

To never lose a loved one!

Spaces Invisible

In a moment lives change

Burst like rainbow bubbles

Bright sun gets clouded over

But we have seen the rainbow

Filling across the horizon

Bubbles rising to the top

In spaces invisible…

Vivid and cheerful—wherever

The memories are held!

You smile your vibrancy

Coming with open arms

Saying "good job" and

I feel your pat on my back

All this… while

I have my eyes closed.

I see you so… vividly

And full of life—wherever

The memories are held!

For Reader Reflections "In Hope"

IN FAITH...

Lift Me Up

You lifted me up, God

Every time I fell...

Raising me up to

Steeper higher pinnacles

Showing new horizons

That I never knew

Existed *within* me...

Go Any Distance

I will go any distance, if

I can see you one more time…

Keeping up the faith

We fervently upheld, striving

I am forward – as promised,

Seeking peace, always!

Holding On

Did I jump in?

Or did I get pushed?

Does it matter anymore?

Really—when I am alone

Neck deep in cold water!

All I know for sure

Is that I don't know

A thing about swimming

Yet, bright as daylight

Flickers the thought:

I want to LIVE!

Does it matter anymore that

I don't know how to swim?

All I want now

Is to live another day!

Hold that thought…

A floating log

An edge of a rock

Slippery as it may be

Will let me see another day!

Holding on… I'll tread

The rising waters: Lord, my GOD…

Is my rock and my light!

Does it Matter

That I can't swim?

Depart I Did Not

Dear, Oh! Dear… my child

Do you not know…

Depart I did not!

Dear, Oh! Dear… my child

Do you not know… I

Dare not leave you!

Dear, Oh! Dear… my child

Do you not feel…

Deep within you, I do dwell?

Dear, Oh! Dear… my child

Do you not hear…

Drumming heart hums, I love you?

Dear, Oh! Dear… my child

Daring feats and challenges

Darling you take upon

Dear, Oh! Dear… my child

Do you not show….

Desired spark of me?

Dear, Oh! Dear… my child

Do I not live through every

Dream of yours?

Dear, Oh! Dear… my child

Delighted heavenly… I'm, when your

Dreams come true!

VeerajaR

On Your Palm

Across the oceans, my GOD—You took me

Amidst strange lands, life You brought me

My biggest dream for me to fulfill

Thy grace lifted me up the hills!

Roaring thunders turned to lullaby

Rampant tornadoes passed me by

On Your palm You hold me, Lord

In my heart Thy words pulse loud!

A Divine Play

I see a playful child with a kaleidoscope

Laughing nebulas as he turns it

Admiring the essence of intricacy

Spurring marvelous living designs

Each color intertwined anew

Every moment in creation.

I see a desolate child with a kaleidoscope

Crying rains as he watches

Flooding the evolving designs - sadly

Spooling in violence and ego

Every color piercing another

Each moment in destruction.

I see a hopeful child with a kaleidoscope

Smiling rainbows as he reigns

Forgiving his prize design - Mercy

Flowing over mankind, reviving

Each heart to love another

Every beat to Peace pronounce.

One More Day

One more day... I pray, loving God

One dear soul to spare... my God!

One more day... to be with her

One more word, I yearn to hear

One more laugh yet to share

One more recipe yet to prepare

One more wild-bird to watch together

One more hug to cherish forever!

One dear soul to spare… loving God!

One more day... I pray, Dear God!

For Reader Reflections "In Faith"

VeerajaR

IN RUAH

Upon Butterfly Wings

Proclaimed upon headstone, dead

You shall breach through

Flesh and bones…

Riding upon the Rainbows bent

You shall weave through

Colors of light…

Perched upon butterfly wings

You shall breeze through

Heaven and earth…

Crouched upon stacking years

You shall brave through

Life for now!

Living Spirit

Yes, I believe

That I will rise - though

My bones may…

Lie beneath the earth

With my last breath…

My soul shall rejoin

The breath of GOD!

Yes, I believe…

Beyond the universe

From alpha to omega

I shall enjoy eternity

In all and in nothing

I shall live a witness… to

The breadth of GOD!

Awaits A Healing Grace

A purpose and place

For

Everyone and everything…

Awaits along life's terrace

At

Every step and every turn,

To arrive and embrace!

Another day with solace

For

Every wound and every mind…

Awaits a healing Grace

For

Every soul—a prize everlasting,

At last to rest, beyond… life's race!

Up On A Pedestal

Please, let me… Oh! God, to
Put my mother up—on a
Pedestal, made of the
Purest gold… Adorn it with
Precious gems of Ceylon, and
Poetry garlands strewn on
Pouring love from my heart!

Please, grant me… Oh, God!
Poetic words melting like
Prime milk chocolate, solid as
Pure gold… glistening smooth.
Picking her out of all angels
Placing in her womb, You blessed…
Poor soul like me, forever!

In My Silent Peace

I have traveled long distance

Yearning for Your silent voice

Searching for Your holy face, my GOD!

I have tried hard, to keep my pace

In this worldly race – holding on

To my faith, Your grace

All I see now… is Thy holy face

Breathing in Your solace

Hearing You loud in my silent peace!

In Ruah

The snow doesn't freeze me

The wind doesn't chill me - now

That I am the snowflakes

And as pure!

The ripples in cold wind

And as free!

Though my bones… lie

Beneath the ground

Thousand stars lift my wings

And I, in *Ruah!*

All Is Well

All is well with the world

While I lie in my hammock

Watching the squirrels chase

With noble intensions, or

Listening to Blue Jay cry

Loud concerns for his mate!

All is well with the world

When the sky is clear blue

Wearing the whitest clouds – and

Air is laden with rainbows of scents

A map for bees and butterflies

Dancing under the hot sun!

All is well with the world

When I can lie in my hammock

Still as a firewood, that…

Cardinal cloaked bright and red, at

Arm's length, sits and whistles

Endless love for his plain old wife!

All will be well with the world

When I lie in my little grave…

Just as I am now,

Resting in my hammock – amidst

A busy world breathing, and

Breeding, happiness all around!

For Reader Reflections "In Ruah"

VeerajaR

AUTHOR NOTES*

Good Morning In GOD (page 2)

A prayer poem I wrote in 2009, and still continues to receive requests from my friends for permission to share with others.

The Lost (page 37)

Written in despair and in memoriam of all the lives lost at Sandy Hook Elementary in Newton, CT, on Dec.14, 2012.

The Loss: A Mother's Cry (page 55)

This poem was previously published (2012) in the Anthology titled "Filtered Through Time," edited by Dr. S. R. Lee

Holding On (page 70)

Inspired by the amazing faith shown by a writer-friend of mine facing cancer ordeal and chemo-drips.

One More Day (page 79)

This is another prayer poem I wrote on Mothers' Day, 2009, when my mother-in-law, Lily Agnes was in a coma, continents away.

Prayers do get answered: I got to read this poem to her in person and laugh together.

Upon Butterfly Wings (page 84)

One of the verses was inspired by the recent book by Dr. Eben Alexander titled "Proof of Heaven."

Up On a Pedestal (page 91)

A memoriam to my mother, Jessie (nee Rajanayagam).

In *Ruah* (page 95)

This poem was inspired by the Hebrew word "Ruah" which means 'wind, the breath of God or Spirit.'

COVER INSPIRATION

Thanks to butterflies that visited our butterfly bush by the porch—for the inspiration and joy they brought me.

COVER GRAPHICS & BOOK DESIGN

Courtesy of…

VeeraMahal Consulting,
Franklin,
TN 37067

THANK YOU FOR YOUR BLESSINGS...

ACKNOWLEDGMENT

For the comradeship and enthusiastic encouragement: Writers' Critique groups of the former Council for the Written Word (CWW) and the Williamson County Public Library (WCPL), the Arts Council of Williamson County, Authors Circle, Franklin FaithWriters and Women's National Book Association (WNBA)-Nashville Chapter.

For cheering me on in my creative endeavors: *My late mother,* Jessie (Uduvil, Ceylon); *My children* – Deepan, Jeevan and Nethraja (US), *my very creative little niece* – Dhanursha Kumarasiri (AU) and *my youngest nephew* – Sachin (SL); *My first creative writing pal and brother,* Premalal (AU); *My grandfather and role model of compassion, late* Dr. Solomon S. Rajanayagam (SL & Malaysia); *My childhood friends,* Dr. Thulasi (CA), Pathmini (AU), Kirupa (SL); *My motivating friends in the creative realm* - Lena Aries, former Director, Nashville Centennial Arts Center; Janice Keck, the late Director, WCPL; V. Clausi, Assoc. Director, Bennington Writing Seminars; L. D. Colln and S. R. Lee, PhD., Published authors and mentors.

For the beautiful nature—

Boundless Beaches, Rolling Hills and Falling Waters that continue to stir up my creative spirits: *Ceylon*, my motherland and *Tennessee*, my current home.

VeerajaR

VeerajaR

A Thank You Note

Below is the most genuine cue—from a guest attending one of my "Paintings & Poetry" exhibitions held in Tennessee, that it's time to publish my poetry collection:

Note From VeerajaR's 'Paintings & Poetry' Exhibition (2010) Guest Book:

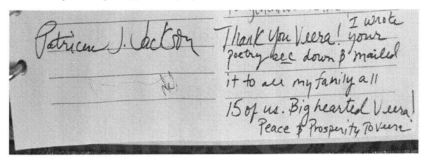

I do not think Patricia Jackson (as signed above) and I ever met, but I'm very humbled to read her genuinely joyous comment that my poetry was precious enough for her to painstakingly hand-copy one by one and share.

It is my hope that this book and the poems bring such joy and peace to all who read them...

May you be strengthened in faith and trust in GOD!

With Best of Wishes,

VeerajaR

21462600R00081

Made in the USA
Charleston, SC
20 August 2013